# GLOBAL WARMING
## A to Z

William Dandurand

Pictures, put in alphabetical order, that have a relationship to Global Warming. It is up to the student to study and reflect on such relationships. It will take all of us to find a way to stop Global Warming, this may be a small step in the right direction.



**ISBN:** 9798524777959

# A

## Automobiles

# B

## Buildings

# C

## Chemical Plants

# D

## Deforestation

# E

## Environment

# F

## Forest Fires

# G

## Greenhouse Effect

# H

## Heat

Annual ocean heat content compared to average (1993-2019)

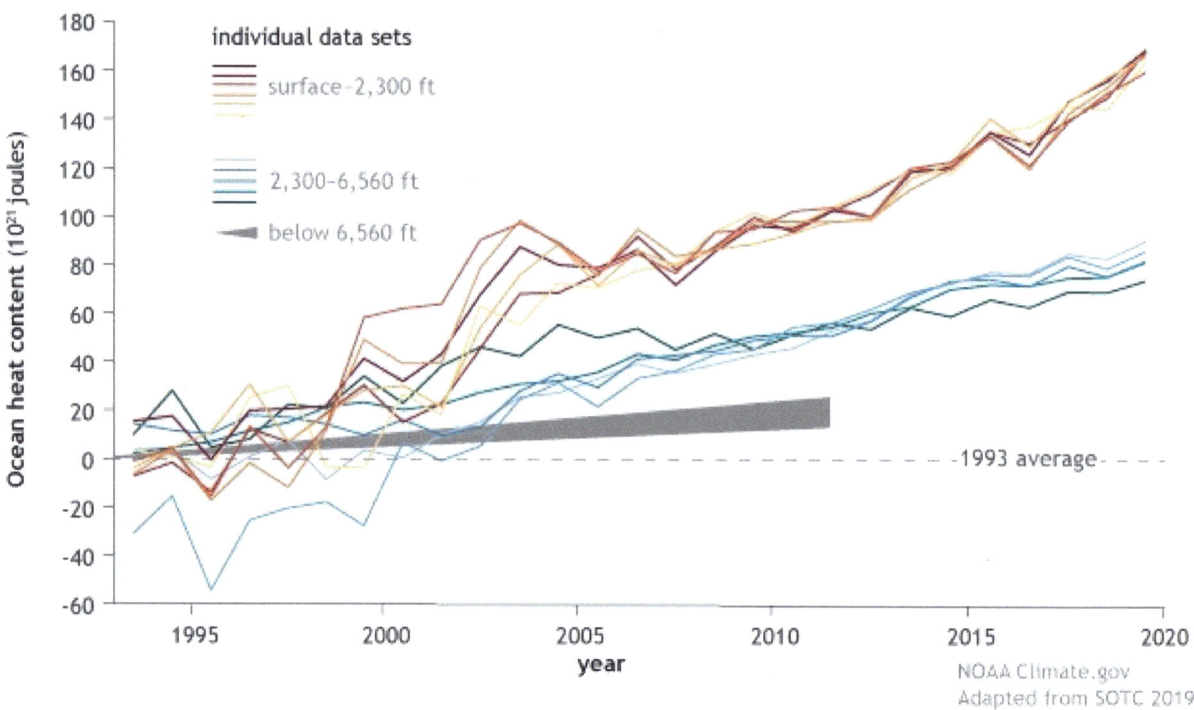

# I

## Industrialization

# J

## Jet Airplanes

# K

## Knowledge Decrease

# L

## Livestock

# M

## Melting Glaciers

# N

## Nitrous Oxide

# O

## Oil Well

# P

## Power Plant

# Q

## Quarries

# R

## Road Construction

# S

## Shipping

TERMINAL BURCHARDKAI
HHLA
HHLA
Hapag-Lloyd
HOUSTON EXPRESS
HAMBURG

# T

## Thawing Permafrost

# U

## Unsustainability

# V

## Volcano

# W

# Wild Fires

# X

## Xtreme Weather

# Y

## Yield Reduction

# Z

## Zizzling